Tips on Ugandan Culture

A Visitor's Guide

Shirley Cathy Byakutaaga

TOURGUIDE PUBLICATIONS
Kampala

Published by
Tourguide Publications
P.O. Box 488, Kampala, Uganda
Email: info@tourguide-uganda.co.ug

Distributed in Europe, North America and Australia by African Books
Collective Ltd (ABC), Unit 13, Kings Meadow, Ferry Hinksey Road,
Oxford OX2 0DP, United Kingdom.
Tel: 44(0) 1865-726686, Fax:44(0)1865-793298.
E-mail: abc@africanbookscollective.com
Website: www.africanbookscollective.com

ISBN: 978-9970-637-03-4

Contents

Acknowledgement

I thank Glenda Jonis Schutger who insisted I write this handbook after I gave her and her husband a short course on cross-cultural adaptation in Uganda in 1992, and Makerere University Institute of Language lecturers, Ms Jane Alowo, Dr Kasalina Matovu (RIP) and Ilona Taute for their encouragement, advice and great ideas.

I thank Ronald Kassimir Akiiki, a Fulbright Scholar, who was my first Rutooro student from America. Ronald helped me discover many things about my language that I had taken for granted.

My thanks go to Lizzy Nazer, a visiting student from UK, and Mathew Udziela and Seth Berez, who contributed the American perspective. Special thanks go to Mr Alestree Fisher, visiting lecturer to Makerere University from UK who did the initial editorial work (any later modifications and omissions are mine). Ed Hobson thanks for recommending a humorous flavor to the book - it has given it a tremendous effect!

Ms Fridah Katushemererwe, thank you for your secretarial expertise.

My dear husband Sam Adyeri and all the S's – you are great morale boosters!

And to all the different development workers from America, Austria, Denmark, participants from Netherlands, UK and Germany, I say, *Mwebale muno! Asanteni, Thank you!*

Preface

My interest in cross-cultural issues started at St. Maria Goretti's Senior Secondary School in Fort Portal, western Uganda. The school was run by American Holy Cross Sisters.

I recall one time, when one of the American sisters waved to a group of local girls and was surprised when, instead of waving back, they ran to her. She asked them why.

"It's you who called us," they said.

"I was only saying 'hello'," she replied.

Apparently, the American wave *"hello"* means "come here" in Uganda! I thought that was strange.

Another time, a nun and a priest (both Americans) set the students giggling when they hugged after evening mass. The Ugandan students were thinking: *"How can a nun and a priest be in love?"*

Uganda is a former British colony and I soon discovered that many words in British English were different from the American English in spelling, idiomatic meaning and pronunciation.

Later, as a student in British Columbia, Canada, I found it strange that people on the bus "buried" themselves in newspapers to avoid talking to each other; or that when I asked for directions to a place, someone simply handed me a map instead of showing me; or that someone became angry when I was five minutes late.

This culture shock made me develop a further interest in this area. Back in Uganda, I started conducting cross-cultural orientations for non-Ugandans and, every time, the same issues came up. So I decided to write this handbook.

This handbook focuses on two major categories of non-Ugandans: visitors intending to stay for short periods, and those planning to stay for longer periods, staying with Ugandan families or working with Ugandans. It discusses the language and socio-cultural practices that foreigners and Ugandans working with foreigners need to understand.

It illustrates Ugandan English, travel language and shopping language, safety tips and non-verbal communication based on real-life experiences of people the author has met through cross-cultural courses, interviews, observations and research.

It is hoped that, after reading this book, you will develop some understanding of Ugandan culture.

You are most welcome!

Webale kwija!

Karibu!

Tusanyuse okukulaba!

S.C. Byakutaaga
August, 2006
Kampala

We and They

Rudyard Kipling

Father, Mother and Me
Sister and Aunties say
All the people like us are We,
And everyone else is They.
And They live over the sea
While we live over the way.
But – would you believe it?-
They look upon WE
As only a sort of They!

We eat pork and beef
With cow-horn-handled knives.
They who gobble Their rice off a leaf
Are horrified out of Their lives;
While They who live up a tree,
Feast on grubs and clay,
(Isn't it scandalous?) We look upon
As a simply disgusting They!

We eat kitcheny food.
We have doors that latch.
They drink milk or blood
Under an open thatch.
We have Doctors to fee.
They have Wizards to pay.
And (impudent heathen!)
They look upon We
As a quite impossible They!

All good people agree,
And all good people say,
All nice people, like Us, are We
And everyone else is They:
But if you cross over the sea,
Instead of over the way,
You may end by (think of it!)
Looking on WE
As only a sort of They!

1

Introduction

Culture shock

When two different cultures come into contact, there are bound to be surprises about the different ways of doing things, and misinterpretations of behaviours and practices.

Misunderstanding is due to each group viewing the other group from its own spectacles and different interpretations of codes. This is termed culture shock.

Your first encounter with Ugandan culture might result in unanswered questions, puzzles to be filled, and frustrations. Your failure to understand or predict what is likely to happen or what is likely to be said may result in embarassing misinterpretations. You need to understand or ask why, to avoid coming to wrong conclusions about Ugandans.

Getting angry about the different ways in which things are done can lead you to say things like, "But that's wrong", "that is not how it should be done", and, "these people are funny".

In order to understand people's behaviour, you have to understand the value system behind the behaviour. You have to understand the historical circumstances that led to that particular value system.

So, every time a new aspect of behaviour is encountered, you need to try to understand it.

But even after understanding the behaviour, you might still not find it agreeable.

That is all right. Your job is not to change the behaviour of Ugandans or to become Ugandan, but to get to know how to adapt to the system and be able to live and work within the system.

Understanding the culture will help you devise coping techniques for smooth co-existence. It is always helpful to think of your culture back home, and pose this question.

"If a Ugandan came to live in my home country, what would appear very 'strange' behaviour? Could she/he change it? How could I advise her/him to adapt to it?"

As you read on, it is hoped that your questions will be answered and you will develop an insight into the different cultures of Uganda.

Is there a Ugandan culture?

The answer to this question can be both "yes" and "no".

Uganda has about 56 ethnic groups and about 30 distinct languages. This means there might be 30 or so different cultures and even more subcultures. A language survey carried out in 1971 identified 63 languages or dialects.

Generally there are many similarities in social cultural practices among Africans in general, and among different Uganda ethnic groups.

But the differences among the ethnic groups make Uganda a "multicultural" society, that is, a culture with various subcultures.

For instance, male circumcision with various rituals, as practiced among the Bagisu, seems to be unique to that ethnic group, while cattle rustling is an "accepted" practice among the Karimojong in the northeast of Uganda.

In western Uganda marriage practices vary between the Banyankore and the Batooro. Batooro men kneel down when asking their in-laws for their daughter's hand in marriage, while Banyankore men do not kneel.

In addition, western influences have taught Ugandans to act in a double-cultured way. For example, when a woman is in the city she might wear trousers, but she will not wear them in the countryside to avoid being looked upon as a prostitute or an indecent person, or as showing disrespect to her in-laws and elders.

Therefore, do not be too surprised when your Ugandan friend behaves in a certain way in the city and differently in the countryside. The multiplicity of cultures is not peculiar to Uganda, but is to be observed in other countries like Kenya, Tanzania, as well as in countries of Asia and the Americas. Thus, the discussion of Ugandan social cultures will be based mainly on similarities; at the same time the special differences will be cited.

Uganda is undergoing significant cultural changes, mainly due to the influences of other cultures from America, Europe and Asia. So, depending on who you meet and talk with, you might get a totally different picture from what is described here.

Time Concept

"We all agreed we will have a meeting at eleven, everyone but I arrived an hour, or even two hours late. Nobody apologised and when they eventually arrived, they wasted more time by greeting and laughing with each other."

The concept of time varies between industrialised and agricultural societies. Whereas industrialised groups view time in terms of seconds and minutes, the agricultural ones view it in terms of seasons, periods or stretches of work routine. Uganda, a country with an agricultural orientation is no different.

Even today people refer to their birth dates in terms of seasons. Someone will tell you she was born during the long dry spell, or in the time of the terrible famine. These habits are even reflected in names given to people - the one born during the drought, the floods, etc. The time used to be estimated by looking at the position of the sun or meaning of the cockerel's crow. The morning, for example, stretches from sunrise to midday. If one has to do some work in the morning, it does not matter if it is done ten minutes to nine or twenty minutes to ten, as long as it is done within that stretch of time. Therefore, most Ugandans fail to understand why people get upset if one is five or ten minutes late. Most people will not even apologise for being late because it does not make sense.

When does night and morning start?

Ugandans count time in terms of daylight and darkness. Being on the equator, there are equal daylight and darkness hours. Thus, for a Ugandan, a day begins at dawn 07:00, which is counted as hour one. 08:00 is the second hour until 18:00 which is the twelfth hour of the day. Then 19:00 is the first hour of the night, and 20:00, the second hour of the night.

Confusion arises when a European says Thursday morning at three o'clock. To a Ugandan this is nine hours on Thursday morning. Those who plan to take "early morning" flights have to be very explicit and double check with Ugandan drivers to ensure both are talking about the same time.

Remember: Not all public clocks tell the right time.
Do not ask about distance in terms of hours it takes to reach a place, due to unreliable transport and other factors it may take a lot longer.

Fluid deadlines: Most "deadlines" will be extended until the task is accomplished. So when you order your furniture, clothes dry cleaning, tailoring, etc, do not expect to receive it on the promised date. This is because due to time concept differences, it is when the task is accomplished that matters, not the time the customer needs his article.

The Fishbowl Effect

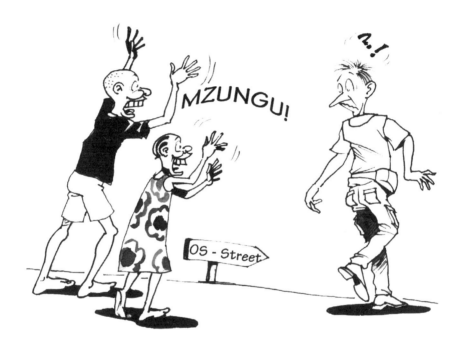

"They stare so much!"
"I hate being called Mzungu all the time."

"The kids! I get pissed off when they say 'how are you Mzungu', following me everywhere saying 'Bye Bye Mzungu!'

"I know that I'm different. I can never be a Ugandan however closely I try to integrate. But calling me Mzungu magnifies it a thousand times. I feel I do not belong here!"

"It depends, if it is on a good day, I respond to them, if it has been a bad day' I feel like..."

These are some of the reactions of people interviewed about how they feel about being called *Mzungu.*

Why are people called Mzungu? Isn't this racial discrimination? Aren't Ugandans very racist?

The author's experience is that, in Britain and America, people pretend not to notice your colour or deformity. However, in Uganda, people "tell it like it is", NO PRETENCE. To identify you, someone might call you the "the fat one", the "old one" or the "brown one". If someone is lame, he/she might be called the "lame one." If someone is blind she will be called the "blind one".

However, all these labels do not carry value judgments. People are simply describing what they see. In Ugandan culture, skin colour doesn't have a value judgment.

In America, South Africa and other countries where racism has been a problem, it is impolite to refer to someone's skin colour.

Not surprisingly, people from such countries conclude that the term *"mzungu"* is racist.

What does Mzungu mean?

Mzungu is a term borrowed from Kiswahili to mean "white person". Different people have heard various definitions and interpretations of this word, such as traveller, or wanderer, referring to explorers who moved from place to place. Today, it generally means "white person". It is pronounced differently in different languages.

In Runyoro-Rutooro – Omujungu
Runyankore-Rukiga – Omujungu

In Luganda – Muzungu
Ateso – Emosugut
Luo – Munu

Is "Mzungu" derogatory?

We can reliably say that most of the time the word Mzungu is not derogatory. In most cases it is used in a hailing manner. Historically, when the Europeans came to Uganda, they introduced many new items that the native people admired, such as cutlery, cars, radios and other equipment that made life more comfortable.

So, the word *Mzungu/Mujungu* was broadened to mean, "leading a comfortable life". Thus expressions like, "you live like a Mzungu" or "You are my Mzungu," meaning my favoured one. Mzungu can also be used to refer to a disciplined, time conscious person.

Attracting attention

Quite often the word *Mzungu* will be used by taxi drivers, vendors and boda-boda people to attract your attention, to buy their commodities or use the services they are offering. Ugandans use terms such as "*Mama baby*" if a woman is carrying a baby or "Mzee" for an old or respected person, or "Mummy!" 'Auntie' to refer to women.

Children will also try to attract your attention by calling you "*Mzungu*" and waving to you.

"What do I do if children follow me around shouting Mzungu, Mzungu?"

It depends where you are and with whom. As mentioned earlier, there is no intention to hurt your feelings. So, tell children that you don't want to be called *Mzungu.* Tell them your name, if you like. If you are working with a group in a village, tell them what you want to be called. This helps them learn about other people too.

When you say "hello" to people and let them know your name, there will be no need for any other identification label. It also enables you to identify with your community.

Why then call me 'Mzungu' if I am black?

What you need to know is that Ugandan skin-colour classifications are different from what you may be used to. For example, in English you talk of blonde, red hair, or blue or green eyes. To the average Ugandan among whites these colour shades do not seem to exist; they are not aware of them; to them all white or light skinned people look the same.

Similarly, when Ugandans talk of a black or brown Ugandan, or one of medium complexion, Europeans, who have not been exposed to blacks, do not find these differences obvious. As the saying goes, *"after all, they all look alike."* So, in America, someone may be classified as an African-American even when their skin colour is almost white, while in Uganda, one may be called a *Mzungu* or a half-caste.

What then does "half-caste" mean?

When Europeans came to colonise, envangelise, and trade, some of them married Ugandans. The result was children of mixed complexion. Such children are called half-castes, or **Bacootara** in some languages.

Sometimes a Ugandan's tribe becomes his/her name!

Someone may be called Musoga because he belongs to the Basoga tribe or Mutooro if he comes from the Tooro tribe.

This is common when someone settles in a place where there are few other people from his tribe. It is not done for discrimination but for identification.

Such a practice, of course, is not very polite; but it is accepted, especially at places where people do not care about learning other's names, such as at taxi parks, and markets.

Some people even call me Negro!

Many Ugandans are unaware of the African-American identity, its African roots or names such as Afro-Americans, Black-Americans, etc. Many don't know that the word Negro is derogatory. To most, it simply means an African American. That is why one may be asked, *"Are you a Negro?"*

The movie industry has added to the confusion about these terms. Many films that are shown here use words such as *"nigger"* in reference to a black person. So, it is important to know that Ugandans use these terms without any intention of racial discrimination. If you experience this, explain the history of this term so that others can learn about it.

Why do people expect me to speak Luganda when I am an African-American?

Language is an identification code. On the basis of your skin colour, the way you do your hair, and look, Ugandans might deduce you are Ugandan so they expect you to speak their language. They think you are one of them.

Many Ugandans, especially young people, want to imitate the accents of American film stars; they want to dress like them, walk like them, etc. So, one sometimes hears people trying to speak American English.

All this makes it difficult to tell whether you are a "true" or "fake" American. If it becomes a big problem for you as an African/American or it's better to emphasise your American identity by how you dress and behave. For instance you can avoid wearing African prints.

I am called Chinese even when I tell them I'm English

As mentioned earlier, Ugandans judge one's nationality by one's looks. If your parents are of Chinese origin and your looks are Chinese, they will not understand if you tell them that you are English.

This is because they see that you have physiological features similar to the Chinese they are used to.

It may indeed be annoying especially if you do not speak the Chinese language let alone know what China looks like. Unfortunately that is the situation. Even Ugandans of Indian parentage are referred to as Bahindi or Bayindi meaning Indians.

Mzungu Price

Why am I charged a different price if there is no discrimination?

One's cultural upbringing and socialisation impacts on how one behaves in different situations, and interpretations of certain behaviours.

In Western cultures, commodity prices are fixed and one does not bother to ask what the price is or bargain, since the price tags are already clearly indicated. When the first Europeans came to Uganda they assumed that here, too, prices were fixed.

It could also be that prices were so low that the Europeans felt they were buying at give away prices. So, whatever price they were told, they paid.

Africans thought, because **Wazungu** were rich, they never bargained, the Wazungu thought that it was the system of trading. This practice has continued to date. It has been extended to Ugandans who are Wazungu (rich) or those who prefer to do their shopping while seated in their cars. However in some shops prices are fixed so bargaining is not practiced.

What you need to understand is that the person who is hiking the price does not see it as cheating but more of being lucky. He will even boast to friends about it as having had his "lucky day" of selling to a **Mzungu**.

Note: Ugandans are roughly 80% right whenever they assume that a Mzungu has more money than they do. But you have every right to refuse to pay the higher price.

Ask your Ugandan friends what a fair price is. That way you can tell if you are being overcharged. Shopping at the same place frequently and speaking the local language also identifies you as "resident" and not a tourist. That helps.

Bargaining is acceptable, especially with open air vendors. Offer half of the price or even a quarter. Before going shopping, try to find out about price ranges from newspapers or visit supermarkets where prices are fixed.

Such surveys will help you get a good bargain from vendors.

Cross-cultural Practices and their Interpretations

Food Matters

Prayers

"I was already eating when he said, 'let's pray'. Does this happen often?"

Most Ugandans pray at mealtime, so expect a short prayer before a meal in most homes. It is a Christian practice introduced by the British and French missionaries. Whites are, especially, assumed to be Christian and, therefore, to pray.

Clearing my plate

"They kept filling my plate until I just had to stop eating! What do I do in such a situation?"

When you visit a Ugandan home you will be served a meal. Traditionally, it is impolite, embarrassing, and uncomfortable for the host if her visitor is not fed.

You do not have to eat all that you are served.

Leaving food on the plate shows you are full and cannot eat any more, which pleases the host. It is interpreted as a sign of satisfaction.

Uganda is blessed with an abundance of food and in many areas people can afford to throw away food.

This practice is changing due to economic pressures but many people still observe it.

In some Western European cultures the way one arranges the knife and fork on the plate shows whether one has finished eating or wants more. In Uganda, depending on where you are, you might want to leave a morsel of food to signal your satisfaction.

Hand washing

"I am not used to being waited upon, let alone being helped to wash my hands before eating."

Most Ugandans do not use forks and knives to eat and believe that staples like matooke and millet cannot be tasty when eaten with cutlery.

So everyone washes their hands before meals, especially when they are to eat with their hands.

But the kitchen is usually out of bounds to visitors. In an average Ugandan home there is no sink available. A young boy or girl pours water out of a jug for everyone to wash their hands in a small basin before and after a meal.

This is typical in rural homes.

It could also be for hygienic reasons: If you hold the handle of the jug and pour out water, the handle may not be clean. It is better for another person to do it so that you remain clean.

"Would it be offensive if I offered to do it myself?"

Although you may offer to pour water yourself, the host would not allow it. It would not be polite. However, after living with the family for some time, you could be left to manage on your own.

Eating with hands

"I was given hot food to eat with my hands, the soup ran down my arm and everybody was laughing at me. I was quite embarrassed."

When you visit a Ugandan home you will be invited to wash your hands so that you can eat with clean hands. Eating with hands can be tough on many foreigners, especially ensuring that the soup doesn't run down one's arm and soak one's clothes. This comes with practice. You could let your host know that it is your first time eating with your hands and ask him/her to help you learn the skill.

Offering something to eat

"How do I offer a drink or something to eat?"

In most African cultures, and Uganda in particular, a visitor is always given something to eat or drink. There are, however, things that cannot be served to any visitor. For example, water cannot be served to a visitor unless he/she has asked for it.

Usually tea, juice, roasted groundnuts, biscuits and soda are among the snacks that will be served to a visitor who will not stay long enough to eat a full meal.

When one is going to serve you, he will not ask you if you would like to have what is to be served, as indicated below:

A: *"Would you like something to eat?"*
B: *"No, thanks"*

If you heard such a cross-cultural exchange especially if B is a Ugandan, chances are that B wouldn't mind a meal but does not want to be considered greedy.

Generally, Ugandans don't ask if one wants a meal or not before offering the meal.

Asking is interpreted to mean you do not really want to give it away but are just asking in pretence. Therefore the person asked feels embarrassed to say yes even if they want to. It is worse if the offer involves food. The guest is embarrassed by the question.

Instead of a question, make a statement: "Have something to drink or eat" or, if you are offering a variety say, *"I have A, B, C, which one would you like?"*

Coffee, tea, and sugar

I said, "I don't take milk and any sugar in my tea and everybody was surprised. Is this offensive?"

Generally, unless for health reasons, Ugandans serve their guests tea with milk and sugar. A guest is served black tea if the host has run out of milk.

Black tea is taken either when one cannot afford milk or for health reasons.

Note: Black tea is also called "dry tea"; it may also mean coffee without milk.

So not taking either milk or sugar or both in your tea could surprise the host.

If you are hosting ensure that you serve tea with milk and sugar, as some people might turn down black tea.

In addition, Ugandan tea is relatively bitter compared to Earl Grey and other teas.

Sugar and milk are favoured because for many Ugandans, tea is the only way to drink milk. Most Ugandans do not drink plain milk.

The slogan "Any time is tea time" holds true in Uganda. So even on a hot day you might be served hot tea. It is believed that you cool off better after drinking hot tea. Hot tea also assures you that you are drinking safe boiled water.

In areas where cows are kept, plain milk or tea with a high concentration of milk is served. Milk tea is normally half water and half milk.

Meat

Meat is a delicacy in Uganda. It is usually served to show a host's politeness and standard of entertainment. As mentioned earlier, people cannot/ ask you if you eat meat or not.

They assume you do. Asking could also be interpreted that the offer is not genuine. Vegetarians are pitied and, in extreme cases, herbal medicines are offered so that you can also start enjoying meat! Health or religious reasons for avoiding meat are more acceptable here than animal rights.

Note: green vegetables are not commonly served as people associate this with poverty, or if a dish is served, it will be in very small portions.

Chicken: The gizzard is for the guest

Chicken is an even greater delicacy than meat among various tribes such as the Baganda and the Bagisu. If you are served with chicken in areas where it is a delicacy, this shows that you are a very honoured guest. The gizzard, which is the most favoured part of the chicken, will be served to the chief guest. When there is no chief guest, the head of the home is the one who eats it. This is usually the father. Do not feel shy about mentioning it to your host if you are not a gizzard fan. Just say you feel honoured but won't eat it.

Grasshoppers (ensenene)

Grasshoppers are a delicacy among various tribes in Uganda, for instance, the Batooro, the Banyoro and the Baganda.

Traditionally, women did not eat them but now many do. The wife in a home was expected to catch grasshoppers for the husband. The husband would, in turn, have to buy a dress in appreciation; if he did not, she would report him to his parents and he would be fined heavily. In some rural areas this is still practiced. Thus, if one takes the trouble to give you "ensenene" it shows they hold you in high esteem.

Funeral Matters

"What should I do if I am invited to a funeral?"

Do not wait to be invited to the funeral of a workmate or neighbour. Death and sickness are instances where any member of the community is expected to participate without invitation. No invitation is ever given for such occasions. Neighbours, friends and workmates are expected to visit the bereaved and extend condolences. Your visit doesn't have to be long but your presence shows that you are touched by the death and you are feeling with the people.

As in most African cultures, death in Uganda is attributed to an "evil eye".

The Banyoro in western Uganda, for example, say, *"Omuntu tayefeera"*. The expression means "a person cannot die without cause" and implies foul play in every death.

Death is attributed to sorcery, misfortune and the spite of the neighbours. So, if a person dies and a close neighbour does not visit the bereaved, they might be held responsible for the death of that person. Even if you did not get on well with the deceased, make yourself seen, otherwise you may be mistaken for rejoicing upon the death.

"I was surprised when people came asking who had died after I made a fire in front of my house."

As in many cultures, breaking the news of death is difficult for Ugandans. Lighting a fire in front of a house signals that death has occurred. So some people could interpret lighting of a fire in one's yard as an announcement of death. Among the Batooro, the fire is lit at the main entrance to the house if it is the head of the family who has died.

The fire is lit to the side if any other member of the family dies. A vigil is kept every night and the fire keeps insects away. In most cases the men stay outside at the fire while the women remain inside the house with the body.

The fire is kept burning for three days, if it is a female who has died, regardless of the age; and for four days if it is a male who has died.

Dress is another way of showing bereavement. In Buganda women add a wrapper on top of the gomesi and tie it in a different style. The lesus or *kangas* are wrapped around the waist by women when going to burials.

"Should I allow my employees to attend funerals, they have so many relatives?

Family ties are very strong in Africa and Uganda.
Every member of the same clan is considered a relative because it is believed they have the same ancestor.

Ugandan families are fairly big compared to Chinese or Europeans families. On average, a small family in Uganda may have six children. When each of the children has six children, the first cousins will number thirty-six. These cousins are very close relatives. In fact, most Ugandan languages don't have a word for cousin. Cousins are also called brother or sister.

Family members are expected to support each other financially and materially, so attending funerals and weddings is very important.

One would rather miss a wedding than a funeral.

Due to economic constraints, a Ugandan may not be able to attend all the funerals. He will send an apology and visit the bereaved after some days.

Missing burials continuously could result in disciplinary action by relatives.

It is best to negotiate with your staff how to deal with this matter, given the frequency of deaths in Uganda.

In case of the death of a member of staff or a member of his/her nuclear family, most organisations provide a coffin and transport for the body to the place of burial.

"Am I expected to attend the funeral of my employee and those of his/her relatives?"

The employer is expected to participate in the funeral of an employee. Always prepare to give a speech or a eulogy even without prior notice.

Alternatively, the organisation could send a representative to an employee's funeral. You do not have to participate in the funeral of a relative of your employee.

"Why do people collect money when someone has died?"

The money collected when someone has died is called **amabugo** in most languages.

The money is meant to help the bereaved family meet the cost of transporting the body, feeding mourners, funeral expenses, and paying the fare for relatives who should attend the burial but cannot pay their way.

Mourning lasts at least three days and can be costly.

Every member of the community is expected to contribute **amabugo**, but it is not compulsory. It is given as a token and sign of sympathy for the bereaved family.

In Ugandan cultures, it is believed that the dead do not disappear completely.

That is why people would want, whenever possible, to bury their dead in their ancestral home. Bodies are also often kept in the house so that people bid the dead a proper farewell. In the African traditional religion, ancestors would be prayed to, and food and drink would be shared with them. Unfortunately Christians have labelled the practice satanic.

26

Relationships and Social Behaviour

Thank You/please

"Don't Ugandans ever say 'thank you' or 'please'? They are always ordering people give me this, take that, eat this!"

Almost all the languages of the world have ways of expressing politeness. The way it is done differs. English uses 'please' to request. Many Ugandan languages, however, use a change in the intonation to express politeness. Someone expecting the word "please" might not easily detect the change in intonation.

Also, when a polite expression in the mother tongue is directly translated into English it could sound impolite. For example, in the Bantu languages if one said mpa sente with a softer tone on mpa the sentence would be very polite. But when the same form is translated into English it becomes *"give me money"* which is an order in English.

A number of westerners fail to detect the politeness tone used by Ugandans speaking English. This may result in misunderstanding.

The author witnessed such an incident. While traveling by taxi, the conductor started collecting the fare from the passengers. In Luganda he kept saying **Leeta Sente.** He sounded polite.

However, when he came to a ***Mzungu*** gentleman in the taxi, he switched to English. This is what happened:

Conductor: I want your money
Mzungu: What for?
Conductor: Give me your money
Mzungu: … Please, Please
Conductor: (Conductor backs off but after ten minutes returns) I want your money.
Mzungu: Say please!
Conductor: (Confused) Bring your money
(Author intervenes and explains to the conductor: "She is saying that when you are asking for her money you should say, "Please".
Conductor: I want your money please
Mzungu: (Hands over the money)
Thank you

All languages of the world have a way of expressing appreciation. Apart from the word for "thank you" the way it is done may vary from language to language. For example, among the Batooro one expresses thanks after a meal but among the Baganda it is done before and after a meal. In some Ugandan cultures, there are also various things which are not supposed to receive thanks in some Ugandan cultures. Things such as water, medicine, seeds are among them. Among Banyankore one is not expected to say thank you for a meal. In fact if one says "thank you" after a meal you are politely reminded that you never say thank you for food. Instead you could say "you have cooked well." Similarly, in some cultures, one may express thanks when offered a seat. Yet in others, if a seat is available you take it without its being offered, because it is impolite to talk with someone while standing.

The instances of expressing thanks and applicable etiquette vary from group to group. You need to observe body movements for expression of thanks.

Family

"There are so many fathers, mothers, sisters and brothers that I sometimes think I am being fooled about their relationship."

The term *"extended family"* is not used in Ugandan languages to describe a type of Ugandan family. The typical Ugandan family includes the parents, uncles, aunts, grandparents, cousins, nieces and nephews.

In most Ugandan languages the word for 'cousin' is brother or sister; the word for 'nephew' is son, the word for 'niece' is daughter, for 'uncle' it is father and for 'maternal aunt' it is mother. These terms show the close ties that exist in traditional African families.

In some ethnic groups, if one referred to a nephew as my "sister's son" instead of "my son" it would be discriminatory. Western influences are however changing the practice.

Even clansmen and clanswomen are part of the family although they may not be living in the same place. Someone from Kabale (southwestern Uganda) could go to Bugisu (eastern Uganda) and on finding a person from the same clan treat him or her as a relative, that is, someone who, along the line, must have the same ancestry.

Relationships of kinship come with responsibilities and duties to be performed by the family members especially in times of crisis such as sickness and death.

Family members are expected to provide moral, physical and financial support to the afflicted.

The Rutooro proverb, **Abaingi banobwa atuubire** (meaning that, "It is only the greedy who dislike having many people around) exemplifies the appreciation of big families.

The elderly, such as grandparents or great-grandparents, also have a major role in the family, and community. The grandmothers baby-sit the grandchildren, playing with them, singing and telling them folk tales and jokes. Such roles have diminished in urban families.

Marriage
Senga (aunt)

The paternal aunt, called **Senga** in Luganda, has the role of rearing up her niece to show the best behaviour. She carries out all the customary rites of initiation into marriage and explains to her niece to show why she must keep her virginity until marriage. She chaperons her and could introduce suitors to the girl's father.

Some of these roles have either changed or are not being as strictly followed today as they used to be in the past.

Omuko (in-law)

The son-in-law or *omuko* in Luganda and Runyoro-Rutooro, is respected by his wife's family. In some cultures, like the Baganda and the Batooro he cannot eat at the same table with his mother-in-law. This is because, in the early days women married when they were very young, when the in-laws were still young and attractive. Such restrictions ensured that the son-in-law did not become attracted to his mother-in-law.

To enforce observance of such cultural practices, superstition emerged such as the claim that when a woman ate at the same table as her son-in-law, her hands would shake, or if she shook hands with the son-in-law she would develop a rash. All these were designed to discourage any physical contact.

Some families still observe these practices strictly. It is important to know how to behave in such a situation, if you have Ugandan in-laws.

Children

"I don't like children and everybody knows that!"

This will be one of the most surprising statements to any average Ugandan's ear! (It shocked the author when she was in Canada, reading advertisements classified for accommodation, where it said "pets yes but no children." She read it over five times but could not understand how a dog or cat could be preferable to a human being! On inquiry, various explanations were given to her about the restrictions applicable to different areas of accommodation.

In Uganda children are treasured. Mostly they are expected to be seen but not heard.

Children are expected to offer security for the parents in their old age.

In many Ugandan societies childlessness is taken as a curse and in many cases the woman takes the blame for it. A couple will try very hard to get a child. Among the Bakiga, a childless woman would not be buried in the same way as one who has had children. Instead of taking her body out through the main entrance, it is taken through the side one or the back door. This practice has been condemned and is beginning to change.

Children used to be the responsibility of the community. Any member of the community would reprimand a child found misbehaving.

Changes in cultures have led most parents to expect no one but their children. In such cases, any misbehaviour is reported to the parents who take action.

Children are expected to participate in housework, mainly fetching water, collecting firewood, looking after animals and caring for their siblings.

Where families can afford house-help, a lot of this work is left to the house-help and the children are left to play or do their school homework. Many children still provide labour in many Ugandan homes.

Privacy
Is there any privacy in Uganda?

"Never have I had any privacy since I came here! I want to be alone!"

"Not even my boyfriend could understand that I needed to be alone. ALONE, that's it."

Uganda is a communal rather than individualistic society. This means there is a lot of interdependence in the family, clan, tribe and work place. In individualistic cultures, the individual matters more than the group.

The communal way of life makes the typical Ugandan view of privacy different from the western.

In some cultures, privacy means being alone and not talking to anybody.

Someone might want to be alone if they are sick or wish to meditate.

Ugandans will assume you want to be with other people when you are sick or upset. If someone falls sick, friends and relatives feel they should visit that person to provide company and comfort.

It is very unusual for someone to say they want to be alone. People will wonder why and ask questions.

So when visitors want to be alone, some hosts think they are lonely and try to offer them company. It helps to let your hosts know that moments of privacy are important to you.

It is rude to send visitors away from your house, even though visitors could arrive unannounced and stay for a long time.

Friends, especially, assume they can visit you any time.

"Are there any areas considered private, areas where I should not go in one's home?"

In the west, the host usually shows the visitor the geography of the house, but in Uganda it is normally the sitting room, dining room and toilet and bathroom to which a visitor has access. The kitchen and bedrooms are normally private. It is usually up to the guest to ask where the toilet is and he is shown where it is. Many Ugandan women do not like visitors, even their husbands going into their kitchens. So a kitchen is considered private.

Personal Space

"I was used to having my personal space but it is so difficult here. There always seems to be space for one more person on the taxi."

Different cultures have different ways of using and defining personal space. For some cultures, the closer one is to you, the better one displays his attention and interest in what you are saying.

For other cultures "too close" is extremely uncomfortable. For example, North Americans seem comfortable with a distance of about 50 cm in normal conversation, while Ugandans are confortable being very close to each other especially in queues.

Due to communal life, close family relationships, and large families, use of personal space in Uganda is different from that of the west. Children in a home share a bed, playing space, and personal property. The personal space concept is determined more by the situation, but generally 'too close' is acceptable.

On taxis and buses, the "personal" space issue refers to only where one is "seated". When boarding a bus or queuing at the post office, very little space is left between people lining up, depending on the demand. In fact if "too much" space is left between the people in the queue another person is likely to come and use it up so that it is not "wasted".

Barricaded houses

"Why does each house have to be barricaded? It scares me, in case of a fire."

In the countryside homes have temporary or no fences to demarcate the boundaries.

In some areas, the doors remain open the whole day and one can leave clothes out on the line to dry.

It is different in urban areas. People feel insecure.

A history of moral degeneration, resulting in thefts, corruption and killing is the main reason people put up wall fences to protect themselves and their property.

It was during the dictator, Idi Amin Dada's regime that wall fences appeared in Kampala.

Today many affluent homes have a wall fence and iron bars (burglar proofing) for security reasons and even as part of the decoration of the house's surroundings.

Ensure that keys to the different locks are kept separate in specific places. If you prefer one bundle of keys, mark them for easy identification. Have an exit plan in case of an emergency.

Trespassing or maintaining friendship?

"Many people trespass on my compound; they seem to have no sense of private property!"

In most villages, footpaths run from one person's house to another. So passing through someone's yard is not looked upon as trespassing by most Ugandans.

Such an act might, in fact, be seen as a sign of good neighbourliness.

It is also important for effective sharing of information by word of mouth. The absence of an over-used path between neighbouring homes is a sure sign that the neighbours do not get on well.

It is important to have paths to neighbours' houses because ones neighbour is considered a very important person in Ugandan communities.

Fencing off your property is an option, but it is important to note that in some Ugandan languages the word for 'fence' translates as "prison".

Fencing is only for keeping families together but not for keeping trespassers out.

House-help/domestic Help

"I find it extremely difficult to employ someone as my househelp or to send them to do something for me, because I am not used to having a servant. Isn't it condoning slavery?"

Unlike in developed countries, servants are inexpensive in Uganda. For centuries, Ugandans of status have had house help. Jobs are scarce and people seize any source of income. Most domestic servants take jobs to raise financial support for their parents or siblings.

Having servants in the home offers an easy way for outsiders to learn about Ugandans.

It makes it easy to learn a Ugandan language.

Invitations

"I invited about thirty people for a party, only two have confirmed. Do you think they'll come?"

Whereas most Ugandans expect and value invitation cards, they rarely call back to confirm, let alone carry cards with them. In the rural areas it is even worse, because people do not always have access to phones. However, be assured that they will take note of the date and appear for the party. In addition they are likely to come with one other uninvited person.

Remember: When you invite a Ugandan for a meal at a restaurant, you as the "host" are expected to pay all the cost because it is you who extended the invitation. If the meal is at home, guests will not bring any drink or food as contribution, because it is you who is hosting the event. So, always plan to have enough money or food on such occassions.

Dressing

"Why is so much importance attached to dress?"

Appropriate dress is important in many cultures. In some hotels, blue jeans and caps will not be allowed. Inappropriate dress can cause embarrassment.

In Uganda, people love to dress well. If you have nice shoes, a tie and a coat for a wedding then you are smartly dressed. Your host could feel offended if you dress casually for an important ceremony.

The host could feel that you have not accorded the ceremony its due respect.

Ugandans also judge economic status by dress. If a **Mzungu** does not dress smartly it is interpreted as disrespect because it is assumed that he/she can afford good attire.

Some work places have dress codes. Civil service men are supposed to wear long-sleeved shirts, ties and long trousers. Women are expected to wear knee-length dresses or suits.

Formal occasions, like weddings, could have appropriate traditional dress among different tribes. It is important to get information and dress appropriately.

Inappropriate dress includes shorts and T-shirts at weddings or for meeting a government official.

"Is there strict female and male dress?"

The traditional dress for men is a Kanzu, a long flowing tunic. For women, it is **gomesi or suuka** for most of Uganda and western Uganda respectively. Among older people, it is unacceptable for a woman to wear trousers. A woman going to a rural area is advised to wear a long dress because that is the norm.

Compliments

"Aren't Ugandans used to being complimented? I told my friend she has a beautiful baby and she said 'No'!".

Ugandans downplay compliments. Revelling in a compliment is assumed to be a mark of vanity. Ugandans are, however, happy to be complimented.

Pets

"I told them that my favourite cat had died and they laughed!"

Respect for pets in Ugandan culture is rare. Cattle keepers could have a favourite cow.

Such people would become so attached to it that, if the cow died, some would even commit suicide. Dogs are kept to keep thieves away and cats are kept to kill rats in the homestead. But these pets are not held in high regard.

"Why do people attack dogs for no reasons at all?"

In most Ugandan homes dogs are not kept as pets but as guards and for hunting. They are pushed away from people.

There is usually a clash of cultures between Ugandans and Europeans over the treatment of dogs. Europeans think Ugandans are cruel to dogs and other pets while the Ugandans think Europeans pamper them.

Ugandans often fail to understand how one can avoid giving a lift to another person but carry a dog instead.

Interestingly, in many Ugandan communities, dog names are also used to convey messages to others, especially if there are constrained relationships. One can easily call his dog "come in but remember what you did to me".

Roadside "Shock"

"Why do men urinate by the roadside? Do they want to be rude to women?"

This is one of the shocks some visitors experience when they visit different parts of the country.

Urinating by the roadside is not a cultural practice but behaviour that people have turned into a habit.

Sometimes circumstances and the call of nature dictate it. Unlike modern countries that have rest houses along the highways, travellers in Uganda must wait to get to a restaurant to visit a toilet.

Sometimes such facilities are either far away or the restaurant reserves the facilities for its customers.

Roadside shocks result if one does not have money to eat in the restaurant.

It is not that the men want to be rude to the women. In fact women also do it. But they do it some distance away from the roadside and are not easily seen.

The practice is unhygienic and the Ministry of Health has outlawed it. Some towns and local governments are constructing toilets to promote hygiene.

Male–Female Relationships and Other Interactions

Romantic Relationships

"How can I, as a woman, send a clear, unambiguous message that I am not interested in a particular man?"

If you are staying in Uganda for a long time, you will realise that many Ugandans think that white women are "loose". This is because the media, movies, magazines and adverts portray white women as sexy and portray them involved in all sorts of sexual actions.

Depending on where you meet, a Ugandan man could have this impression of you.

Most Ugandan men believe that a man's advances should never be refused or rejected. You will hear phrases such as, "a woman can never say 'yes' the first time" or "for a woman, 'no' means 'yes'".

You need to use many different signals to show that you are not interested in a man. Use non-verbal signals, look him straight in the eye, do not touch him, hug him or kiss him. Do not wink at him (winking sometimes means "I love you").

If it is your colleague, show that work means work.

If you to go for lunch or dinner, invite a third person and, of course, use your instincts to determine whether he is getting the message or not.

"If, as a female, I am interested in a Ugandan man, is it offensive to tell him so?"

As discussed above you should not risk being seen as a "loose" woman. Traditionally, a Ugandan woman could not make sexual advances towards a man. Even now many Ugandan men find it difficult if a woman makes advances to them. Of course, for a woman brought up in a culture where it is acceptable, this is a sign of the oppression of women. Granted. Most men will use you and take advantage of you and even tell others to try their luck if you make sexual advances towards them.

The best thing to do is not to say it verbally. Try to use other means but DO NOT SAY IT.

Dating

"Is it true that parents here do not allow their children to date? What do they have to do with it?"

Dating was non-existent in Ugandan cultures until the arrival of westerners.

Generally, for Ugandans, dating someone or having a girlfriend or boyfriend is interpreted as having a sexual relationship with them.

Bolstered by religion, traditional culture discourages pre-marital sex. It is only the so-called "modern" parents who allow their children to date.

In theory today, therefore, dating doesn't exist but in practice it does. Mostly, however, it is done stealthily. Only a handful of parents openly allow their children to go on dates.

Most parents only acknowledge that their children have been having a relationship when the children seek permission to marry. Parents have a lot of say in their children's marriage affairs.

In the past, parents in some societies, such as Banyoro (western Uganda) would identify the future wife for their son. She would have to be from a family well known to the boy's parents. She would be "booked" for him and at about the age of ten she would be taken to her future mother-in-law who would bring her up in the ways of her future family.

In some areas, if a girl became pregnant outside marriage she would be cast out of the clan. The girl's mother shared in the blame of her daughter's pre-marital pregnancy. This made mothers very protective of their daughters.

In some communities, a young girl on a date would be accompanied by a younger child so that the child could report suspicious incidents to the parents.

Girl-boy friendship or contact was controlled in this way. It was quite difficult for a young boy or girl who were unrelated to meet. But with the coming of formal education and mixed schools, things changed. Girls and boys became more exposed to each other.

Eye Contact

"My girlfriend cannot look me in the eye!"

Most parents tell when their daughter is in love, by watching her eye contact with a boy.

If a Ugandan girl is in love, she will look at everything around her but not in her lover's eyes. She might steal an occasional glance.

It is almost similar in Japan, where direct eye contact is avoided and the area around the neck is what is looked at instead. In many parts of Africa, looking straight in another person's eye is considered rude, more so if it is a child talking to an adult.

Teachers from the west are often frustrated when Ugandan students refuse to look them straight in the eye. Yet the students intend this as a sign of respect. When being corrected, children and subordinates, in particular look down, because looking a superior in the eye is considered a challenge to authority.

Note that for Americans, direct eye contact shows sincerity, interest and honesty.

Some Precautions

Pregnancy

"I asked my colleague when the baby was due, and she was elusive."

Do not ask a pregnant woman when she expects to deliver.

For a man to ask another man's wife when she is expecting is especially unacceptable. The conclusion could be that you are the father of the expected baby.

Only the father of the expected baby asks such a question.

A woman also does not usually ask about the due date unless she is very close to the pregnant woman.

There is a superstition that if someone knows one's expected date, that person could cast a spell on the mother to produce a maimed baby or make the pregnancy disappear.

Such superstitions are changing but the practice of refraining from asking has remained.

Complimenting the beauty of another man's wife

In some cultures, to show politeness to your host, you compliment the beauty of his wife. In Uganda, a man never compliments another man's wife by saying "you have a beautiful wife!" It will not only be shocking to the husband but may also result in other problems. The man could immediately conclude that you are in love with his wife.

Washing your undergarments by another person

"I asked him if he would wash my knickers and he said o.k."

Many people get house help when they come to live in Uganda. Although the house help can do laundry, it is not culturally acceptable at all to make them wash your underwear.

Although your house helper may say it is okay when you ask him/her to wash your underwear, he/she may say it out of fear of losing the job. When other community members learn that the person is washing another ones underwear.

He will be ridiculed and lose respect and self-esteem.

Exposing underclothes to public view

Although the sun is beneficial and freshening to clothes, drying underclothes in the sun where everyone can see them is unacceptable. People are embarrassed to see such clothes on the line. If you must, dry them where they cannot be seen.

People living with Ugandan families should find out from their hosts where they could hang underclothes.

Women sitting with legs apart

In Uganda, sitting with legs together is aimed at preserving the woman's chastity.

Ugandans consider it impolite to show underwear or the inner thigh when seated. Wearing a dress, the proper posture requires the legs to be together. This may be difficult for women from the west who are used to wearing trousers.

Girls in Uganda are trained from an early age not to sit with legs apart.

In the past, women's dress did not include underwear as we know it today.

The underwear was different and if a woman sat with legs apart, her private parts would be visible.

It should be noted that, in many Ugandan cultures, a woman can expose her breast when she is suckling her baby. In some cultures it is obscene and extremely uncouth for a woman to show their breast in public. In some cultures in Uganda, showing one's nakedness in public is a sign of extreme anger. If a woman undresses in anger it is considered the worst curse that can befall those who witness.

Traditional upbringing for girls in most Ugandan cultures emphasises that the girls remain virgins. Girls were not supposed to climb trees, ride bicycles or do things that could compromise their virginity.

A woman fighting with a man

In public and in private Ugandan women have been brought up to control their emotions, especially anger. If a man angers you, it is dangerous to slap him or try to fight him.

In such a situation a man feels challenged, defensive and demeaned and will try to do something to counteract it.

He could therefore become violent.

Public display of affection

Whereas it is acceptable in Europe or America for a man to kiss a woman in public, in Uganda it is not, except at weddings.

People in love who hold hands and kiss in public are considered obscene.

A love relationship is a private affair.

If you get involved in a love affair with a Ugandan, touching and kissing to show love and affection may be interpreted as a desire to make love. This could result in accusations of being sex hungry, uncivilised, aloof and unreserved.

There is a joke about how far apart Ugandan couples behave in public. "If you see a Ugandan man walking 100 metres ahead of a woman, chances are that the woman behind him is his wife."

Usually, if members of the opposite sex holds hands then it is mere friendship, not love. Members of the same sex holding hands has no sexual connotation.

Grabbing one's tie

Grabbing some one's tie is taken as a sign of confrontation. If people are involved in a fight, grabbing another's tie is a sign of trying to strangle him.

Ugandan English and More

Language is dynamic; no language ever stands still. English in Uganda has acquired expressions that are unique to Ugandan English (UE). Below is a list of some of the expressions and their meanings.

Ugandan English		Meaning
1. You are lost!	-	I have not seen you for a while
2. It is sweet!	-	It is delicious
3. It is too sweet	-	It is very delicious
4. To chase	-	To follow up on something
5. I am chasing my cheques	-	Following up the person working on my cheques
6. I don't think	-	I don't think so
7. To supply air	-	Be paid for no deliveries
8. Eaten my money	-	Has spent my money
9. To fluke	-	To gate crash
10. You have a phone	-	You have a phone call
11. Go for a short call	-	Go to the toilet
12. Go for long call	-	Go to the toilet to empty the bowels

13. To soosoo/susu   -   To urinate (nursery
                                 school language)
14. To poopo/pupu   -   To defecate (nursery
                                 school language)
15. To see stars   -   To be confused
16. To bounce   -   To miss somebody
                                 (not find someone at a
                                 place you anticipated
                                 to find him or her
                                 whether on appointment
                                 or not.)
17. I bounced at your house -   I did not find you at
                                 your house
18. To cut   -   Not to attend
                                 intentionally
19. He cuts classes   -   He does not attend
                                 classes
                                 intentionally
20. Zero-grazing   -   Sticking to one sexual
                                 partner
21. To akiibua   -   To run very fast
22. They have knocked me -   Someone has crashed
                                 my vehicle
23. My car   -   A small vehicle
24. He has a 'my car'   -   Someone who has a
                                 personal vehicle
25. You are old e.g you are an old man - You are an adult
26. You are smart! (compliment) - You are very well
                                 dressed
27. Extend   -   Move over
28. To force   -   Put on an accent

29. The guy is forcing - He is putting on an accent

30. You have put on weight - A compliment

31. A soda - A Coke, Fanta, Pepsi etc.

32. Sorry - Expressing sympathy

33. A "see-through" - Transparent clothes

34. To "Kulembeka" - To earn an income

35. To ask for "ebyaffe/ebyaitu"- To claim what used to belong to you

36. Mwanainchi - Citizen

37. A Muyaaye - Badly behaved, idle person, lumpen

38. To crack - To study very hard

39. Ki + Noun e.g. A *Ki* man- A big man

40. Ka + Noun e.g. A *Ka* man- Small man

41. Gu + Noun e.g. the *Gu* man- Huge man

42. Give me on - Give me something for a short while or give part of it (used by the children)

44. To cook the head - To think very seriously, to plan, to strategise

45. To have slim - To be infected with AIDS

46. To look into somebody - To bribe or give preferential treatment

47. To cook something - Make up a story

48. Pick me - Pick up by a car

49. Somehow - Somewhat, sort of

50. A long illness - Euphemism for AIDS

51. Loaded	-	Has a lot of money
52. Welcome back	-	Welcome
53. Yes please	-	Considered to be a polite response 'yes'
54. Are you sure	-	Do you mean it?
55. Are you serious	-	You must be joking! I can't believe it!
56. "Ghost" landlord, teacher etc	-	Non-existent; used for fraud
57. "Just" as in he is talking just	-	Only
58. Well done (Eastern Uganda)	-	Part of a greeting
59. Lousy	-	Lazy, dull
60. have to... e.g you have to go	-	need to, does not necessarily mean it is a must.
61. They are abusing/ beating themselves	-	abusing/beating each other
62. The door has refused	-	the door cannot open
63. The man has jammed	-	He cannot give in, accept, agree
64. I am coming (when *going* in an opposite direction	-	I'll be back soon
65. Are we together?	-	Are you following? Do yo understand?

Market language

Usually when you ask the price of something in markets the prices are repeated. This sometimes confuses people new to this system, as in my experience with Ronald.

Ronald:	-	How much are the tomatoes?
Seller:	-	A hundred, a hundred
Ronald:	-	Here is two hundred shillings
Observer:	-	No, pay just one hundred shillings
Ronald:	-	But she said, one hundred, one hundred, that makes two hundred.

Although prices are repeated, it does not mean that you pay double. It means that it is a certain amount per heap or per kilo. So, "fifty, fifty" means "fifty shillings per measure", or fifty shillings per item.

Prices are usually abbreviated as follows:

One thou (thau)/1K	-	Shs 1,000=
Three thou/3K	-	Shs 3,000=
One five	-	Shs 1,500=
Two three	-	Shs 2,300=
Four eight	-	Shs 4,800=
Five thou	-	Shs 5,000=
One hundred thou	-	Shs 100,000=
Point one	-	Shs 100,000=
Point two	-	Shs 200,000=
Point eight	-	Shs 800,000=

One point two	-	Shs 1,200,000=
One point five	-	Shs 1,500,000=
Four point six	-	Shs 4,600,000=
Five M	-	Shs 5,000,000=
Ten M	-	Shs 10,000,000=

Sometimes the word a thousand is abbreviated to thau). It is advisable to learn these numbers in the local language of your choice. Note that on the different currency notes, the amounts are also stated in Kiswahili.

Pronunciation

"I have told these people I am called 'Brian' but they call me Blian!"

There are distinct differences between Ugandan languages and English.

Whereas English has 12 or 13 vowels, most Bantu languages of Uganda have 5 vowels, while the Western Nilotic languages of Uganda have 10 vowels.

The number of consonants also varies from one Ugandan language to another.

Most Ugandan languages do not have

"th" as in "thin"

"the" as in "these"

"sh" as in "sheep"

Usually a Ugandan speaking English tries to pronounce the nearest equivalent. In some languages the following adaptations will be heard.

Spoken language

Why do many Ugandans like questioning themselves as they talk like... So I did what? I went. In order to what? To finish my work?

In many languages people use a number of conversational cues to keep the listener alert and following what the speaker is saying. In some languages people do a lot of nodding to show that one is following, others use hums and different guttural sounds. In the Ugandan languages, especially in story telling, various tonal changes are used to flavor the story and keep the listener interested. The speaker usually asks those kinds of questions to check whether the other person is still following. The listener may give a response – or the speaker himself usually gives the answer as if it is a rejoinder. If the listener gives the response, then the speaker is happy and encouraged to continue. This style has now been adopted in school teaching as one of the techniques in monitoring whether the students understand.

On the other hand, there are times when the speaker is looking for the right word to say especially in their second or third language, so they use "what" as a filler as they think of the word.

i)   Interchanging (r) with (l) in words: pray and play

ii)   Using (s) "sin" instead of "thin"

iii)   Using (z) "ziz" instead of "these"

iv)   Inserting (d) "diz" instead of "these"

v)   Using (h) before an initial vowel (h), "Handrew" for "Andrew".

vi)   Using (s) 'collecson' for 'collection'

vii)   Using (s) for 'seques' instead of "cheques"

viii) Inserting vowels at the end of words e.g.
comingi (coming), goodu (good) Wanta (want)

Names

Most Ugandans will introduce themselves by saying "My names are .... It does not matter which name comes first. There is no strict order about first, last or middle names. In most formal situations, someone will start with a surname (Ugandan name) Christian or Muslim name, which may be considered the "first name" e.g Banura Moses, Mukasa Karim.

Titles

Most Ugandan cultures refer to an elder or a highly respected person with titles like Sir, Madam, Mzee, Sebo, Nyabo, Mr, Mrs... as a sign of respect.

"Why do Ugandans like to apologise for things they have not done? I dropped a glass and it broke and they all said 'sorry'!"

When someone does something that may cause pain, loss or sadness, the people present are expected to show sympathy. In Luganda they may say "ng'olabye" as a way of showing that you are feeling with the person about the pain or loss, however small it may be. As there is no direct equivalent of these terms in English, the closest is taken as "sorry". So it is not that they are apologising on your behalf, but it is their way of expressing sympathy.

On saying sorry or showing sympathy

One day some children were playing and their ball hit my car – there was no damage but what surprised me -a boy came and picked the ball but never apologized at all!" Is this common?

Usually people apologize if there was a damage or serious inconvenience. However, most of the time if there is no damage, people may not apologize. Reason being that the object is still in its good shape, so it is not necessary to apologize.

Abbreviations

"A" Level	-	Advanced level (high school)
All Saints	-	All Saints Cathedral
Campus	-	Makerere University
Christ the King	-	Christ the King Church
KIU	-	Kampala International University
KPC	-	Kampala Pentecostal Church
MOES	-	Ministry of Education and Sports
MOF	-	Ministry of Finance
MUK	-	Makerere University Kampala
Mulago	-	Mulago Hospital
O' Level	-	Ordinary level (secondary school)
PLE	-	Primary Leaving Examination
Railways	-	Uganda Railways Corporation
UNEB	-	Uganda National Examinations Board
URA	-	Uganda Revenue Authority

Travel language

Ku siteeji	-	At the next stop
Awoo!	-	(Stop there) I want to get off
Zireete	-	Give me your fare
Tugende	-	Let's go, take- off Teekayo
Wofuna parking	-	If you could get parking space (someone wants to get out)
Taxis	-	The public minibuses with a blue and white band
Special hire (special)	-	This is a special rental usually with a black and white band
Abasigadde muziwereze	-	Those who have not paid yet, bring your fare

Place names

Get place names straight. Study your map carefully and note the exact place on a piece of paper. Sometimes your pronunciation may not be correct and you may end up in a different destination.

For example, differentiate between:
*Ka*subi and Kisubi
*Ka*bale and Kibaale
Kaseese and Ka*siisi*
Bu*ga*hya and Burahya

Mb*ale* and Mbarara

Safety Tips

Finding your way

Have you ever felt insecure on the streets of a new town? Have you ever felt people looking at you as if ready to attack you? When you get this feeling, try to find out why. Sometimes it is you who may be making yourself the center of attraction by one of the following actions.

Displaying maps

People stand on the street holding maps confusedly trying to figure out where they are. The moment you do this, you are saying to the whole world, "hey, look, I am new to this city and I do not know my way around".

It is safer to go to an enclosed place, such as a restaurant, bookshop or post office and read your map from there. In this way you lessen the likelihood of being pick-pocketed or mugged.

Inappropriate dress

Your manner of dress is another way of attracting onlookers.

Granted, the weather is very nice and warm and tempting for wearing shorts, but women could be targeted if they over expose their thighs. This will be difficult for some women, because they feel they do not have to dress in a particular way just to please men.

It is a lot safer to protect one's life than ones beliefs, especially when one is in a new environment. In addition, such dressing identifies you as a tourist, thus you will get a different type of treatment – tourist treatment.

Displaying equipment

Some tourists are easily recognised due to the equipment they wear around their neck – cameras, binoculars, video cameras etc. If you carry it, keep an eye and your hand on it, especially in crowds.

Carrying too much luggage

The way you carry your bag may also attract thieves and pickpockets. A small bag should be carried in front of your body, with a hand across it. The backpack should be properly tied and locked.

When traveling on public transport, count the number of bags you carry. It is always better to travel light. Noting down the vehicle numbers is important, in case you forget something on the taxi. You could go to the taxi office and attempt to trace it.

Carrying too much cash

Remember that many Ugandans believe every Mzungu is rich. Sometimes people may carry a lot of cash because they get better exchange rates in Kampala than upcountry. However, this makes you a target of thieves. You would rather change money at a higher rate in smaller quantities, than gain much and lose it all to thieves.

Safety dos and don'ts

- Do not expose your money.

- Do not show that you are frightened or scared or worried that you will be pick-pocketed by looking around at everybody or touching the spot where you keep your money.

- Be confident; act like you know what to do.

- Do not accept easily offered help (use your judgment).

- Do not leave valuables on window sills.

- Do not wear your gold/diamond jewellery on busy streets.

- Do not leave valuables in the car.

- Do not ask people you do not know well if the place is safe for you to leave your valuables.

- Do not accept food or drinks offered on public transport (it may be drugged).

- ~~Do not go to a drinking~~ place alone after dark.
- Move in pairs or bigger numbers.
- Avoid involvement in political debates.
- Do not get involved in a love relationship at first sight.
- Always ask about things you do not understand or you think you understand.
- Keep your windows closed when driving in traffic jams and at traffic lights.
- When driving a pick-up or open truck, make sure everything is securely fastened and be alert at traffic lights and traffic jams as these are areas where your valuables could be snatched.

Use your driving mirror to monitor the back.

- Be extra conscious about the people around you; when you hear persistent honking or horns, others may be alerting you about a thief.

Handy things

- Always carry some toilet paper. It is seldom available in public toilets.
- Carry at least two handkerchiefs. One to dust your face, if you travel, another to use as a tissue.
- Carry some Kleenex (tissue paper). It is available in most supermarkets in Kampala.
- Carry a cap if you are to travel on dusty roads, and to protect yourself from the sun.
- Women should carry a *l*esu/kanga cloth. This is the most wonderful multipurpose wear women can have.

- It can be used as a headscarf when you travel, to protect your hair from dust.

- In case of car breakdown you can use it to sit on as you wait for the repair.

- You can wrap your lesu over your dress to protect your dress from dust (when you get off,the dress the car will still be clean).

- For funerals, women wrap **kangas** around their waist as part of the mourning attire.

Road safety

- Always keep right when walking on a busy road, especially in Kampala. In this way you can see the vehicles coming from the front, because in Uganda we drive on the left.

- Zebra Crossings (crosswalks) are not as safe as you may expect. Be extra careful at zebra crossings.

Green branches

As you travel you may come across green branches dropped in a straight line along the road. In most cases this warns of a problem on the road. It could be an accident or a car breakdown. The leaves are dropped to warn you to drive slowly, especially if it is near a bend. On the other hand robbers could use a similar sign to waylay you. In all cases, you need to be careful.

Electricity

- Uganda uses eletricity at 240 volts.

- To get a step-down converter, check at electric appliance shops and in the Yellow Pages.

- "Load shedding" means your area will have specific days when you will have no power. This will affect your planning; think about alternatives like a generator, charcoal stove, gas cooker or kerosene stove, how much food to buy, and when to cook.

- Two-pin-plugs: You can use this type of plug in a three-hole socket. Get the cover of a Bic pen and insert it in the top hole of the socket by pressing it down. This will force the other two holes to open. Then push the two pins into the two lower holes of the socket.

Non-verbal Communication

Non-verbal communication is another important aspect that needs to be understood when cultures interact. These range from sounds to gesture and facial expressions. Remember that the same gesture may be interpreted differently in two cultures. Always check that the other party shares your understanding of the non-verbal communication.

In the introduction to this book we mentioned that even in Uganda , there are variations in the interpretations of certain words and actions. So ask different people whether you are communicating on the same "wave length".

Vocal Expressions

In Uganda, the different cultural groups sometimes have different interpretations for some of the sounds for example a click type of sound may mean that you are "nobody" among the Banyankore and thus it is an insult. Yet among the Batooro it is contextually-used: it may be an insult in one instance or a sign of marvel or wonder. A "tststs" sound made with the tongue between the front teeth, repeated several times, expresses sadness and disbelief about a sad happening in most of the languages.

"Mm" as if one is humming means 'yes', while "uh uh" or "ah ah" means 'no'. One grunt at the same tonal level means 'yes', while two grunts mean "no", and grunt with a raised tone means "what did you say?"

Someone from a different culture may think that the Ugandan does not want to respond to a question when she says "mmm...". This is because such noise may have a different interpretation in another culture or the person may not notice that such a sound has been expressed.

Laughter

One of the most confusing messages to a foreigner in Uganda is the message given by laughter. Apart from expressing happiness, laughter can also express surprise, wonder and embarrassment.

Smiling is not used as greeting as in some western countries. Sometimes, when a foreigner does something unexpected, such as trying to speak the local language, people will laugh with you. However, some foreigners think they are being laughed at so they take offence. In Uganda people laugh openly, even when it may be embarrassing to the other person.

Hand gestures

The fingers, hands and arms convey a number of different messages depending on the cultures where they are used. The pictures below illustrate some of the messages.

Not for beckoning: Sex sign– Middle finger moved back and forth.

Another sex sign

Waving with an open hand means "hullo" or good-bye.

For beckoning: All fingers are bent and moved back and forth.

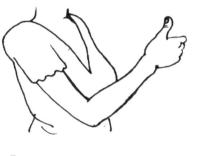

Encouragement: Yeah! thats great.

Snapping: Not for calling human beings. Usually used to call dogs; it can also be used when one is following along with a music tune.

Appendix

According to the Constitution of the Republic of Uganda, 1995 the following are the indigenous communities of Uganda from February 1, 1926.

Acholi	Alur	Baamba	Babwisi
Babukusu	Bafumbira	Baganda	Bagungu
Bagisu	Bagwere	Bahehe	Bahororo
Bakenyi	Bakiga	Bakonzo	Banyabindi
Banyankore	Banyara	Banyarwanda	
Banyole	Banyoro	Baruli	Basamia
Basoga	Basongora	Batagwenda	Batooro
Batuku	Batwa	Chope	Dodoth
Ethur	Ik (Teuso)	Iteso	Jophadhola
Jonam	Kakwa	Karimojong	Kebu
Kuku	Kumam	Langi	Lendu
Lugbara	Madi	Mening	Mvuba
Napore	Nubi	Nyangia	Pokot
Sabiny	So (Tepeth)	Vonoma	